"Fill your paper
with the breathings
of your heart."
William Wordsworth

Business Book Planner

Connect with us

Come and join our thriving community of authors who are taking a similar journey of writing and publishing their books.

Use the hashtag #smartauthorsystem to share your intentions, goals and dreams and let's make your book happen!

Join our Facebook group:
www.facebook.com/groups/authorsjourney

Sign up for the FREE Get Started Workbook: www.librotas.com

Watch the Smart Author Masterclass: www.librotas.com/smart-author

Follow us on social media:

www.facebook.com/librotas

www.twitter.com/librotas

www.linkedin.com/in/karenwilliamslibrotas

www.Instagram.com/karenwilliamslibrotas

Ready to get help with your book?

Visit www.librotas.com/contact or email karen@librotas.com to book a call.

IMPORTANT!

HOW TO BEST USE THIS JOURNAL

- [ ] GET COMFY
- [ ] FIND COLOURED PENS/PENCILS
- [ ] GRAB SOME POST-ITS
- [ ] GO SOMEWHERE QUIET
- [ ] BELIEVE IN YOURSELF
- [ ] TAKE A MOMENT TO BREATHE
- [ ] ALLOW CREATIVITY TO FLOW

#SMARTAUTHORSYSTEM

Dear author

You're here. You're ready. To finally turn your dream of writing your book into a reality. You know that it will transform your life and the lives of your readers. You're ready to step up in a bigger way, to shine the light on how you help others and to make a bigger difference in the world. You're ready to become a Smart Author.

You know you've got a story inside that needs to be told, wisdom that you want to share, advice that will change the lives of others, and a desire to tell your powerful message.

I'm sure that I don't need to tell you that there are so many advantages of writing a nonfiction book or memoir, especially if you're a coach, leader, expert, business owner or entrepreneur.

Your book will be pivotal in your bid to raise your profile, be recognised in your area of expertise, develop your credibility and build your business.

And you'll soon be wowed when you realise the value of what you know, have clarity in your message and are clear on how you can use your experiences to craft your best possible book.

This is your time. So, let me guide you through the 10 principle Smart Author process.

If you've dreamt about your book for far longer than you'd care to admit, or you've felt overwhelmed with the process, by following the guidance in this journal you will quickly discover how to get started and make it a priority.

If you want to make the most of every hour in every day, by creating your plan and following it, you can maximise your time, get rid of any excuses holding you back, and it won't be long before your book is in your hands.

This powerful planning tool takes you through every step you need to follow to get to the end point, with plenty of space to reflect on your ideas. Together we will focus on the areas that are important, so that you don't get distracted by things that could easily get in your way.

And by the time you've completed the insightful questions and exercises in this journal, you will have a clear and powerful outline for your book, a plan of what needs to happen and when, and a place where you can keep all of your ideas and inspiration together.

But I'd like to be realistic too. Writing a book takes time if you want to create your best book. Which means that one of the biggest blockers that holds business owners back is that overwhelming feeling that they should be trying to earn money now, rather than creating an asset that's going to build their future and make a real difference to many people's lives.

So what if there was a way to write a book that self-funds your writing time and pretty much guarantees the content will wow your future readers?

To find out more, I have a surprise bonus for you. I'd like to invite you to watch my free Smart Author Masterclass.

I'll show you how you can write your book in a way that pays for itself and pretty much guarantees it's going to be a raving success from day one. Meaning you'll have the time and headspace to craft the masterpiece your future readers deserve, without feeling hindered by worries about finding clients or paying the bills, or finding a publishing deal.

Plus, in the 60-minute video, I'll tell you how I made £16k from just planning my third book, how one author sold 1,000 copies of her £49.99 book before it was published, and how another gained 132 red hot prospects by simply validating her ideas.

Get instant access at: www.librotas.com/smart-author.

Now if you're wondering why I'm the best person to support you through the journey, let me tell you briefly about myself.

My business journey started in 2006, although everything changed when I wrote my first book in 2009, as it put me and my business on the map. Since then, I've written six books, many of which have been bestsellers, so I know what it's like to go through the process!

Since 2014, I have supported hundreds of coaches, consultants, leaders, experts and entrepreneurs, helping them to go from idea to publication, launch and beyond.

This has enabled them to write books that have built their business, credibility and authority. Plus they have reached far more people than they could have done without their books, allowing them to make a bigger difference and leave a legacy.

Would you like to join them?

Let's get stuck in, explore your ideas and let's make your book happen!

Best wishes
Karen

Karen Williams – The Book Mentor
Librotas
www.librotas.com

Principle 1
Starting with the end in mind

Starting with the end in mind

When you start with the end in mind, you will have a clear idea of what you want your book to do for you, your readers and your business. Without this, it's hard to measure your success, which means that you're likely to fail before you've even started.

That's why the first principle is all about creating the foundations for your book.

In this section, we will start by looking at why you're writing your book, and your personal and business vision, so that you can become clear on how your book will build your business, and what will keep you motivated to get to the end point.

Then we move on to focus on your ideal reader and client. Being crystal clear on who your book is for will enable you to pitch your book in the right way, and ensure that it impacts the lives of the right people.

And if you want to become an authority, you need to niche your book, so that the people who need to hear your message will gravitate towards you. This book may reflect the niche you are in already or reposition you in a new niche if your business is in transition.

This will also enable you to do effective research during the planning stage to find your hungry crowd of people who can't wait to buy your book. I will cover this further in principle 2.

We end this first section with how you are going to leverage your book, so that it becomes a brilliant tool for your business as you write it, when you launch and also in the future.

This is why I am writing my book

Knowing WHY you are writing your book will keep you going when the going gets tough and keep you focused on the ultimate end goal of having your book in your hands.

This is my personal vision for my book

This is my business vision for my book

How important is writing my book on a scale of 1-10?

_____

What are my reasons for this score?

_____

_____

_____

_____

_____

_____

_____

_____

_____

_____

_____

_____

_____

_____

_____

_____

What will my book give me that I don't have already?

_____
_____
_____
_____
_____
_____
_____
_____
_____
_____

What will I see, hear and feel once I've published it?

_____
_____
_____
_____
_____
_____
_____
_____
_____
_____
_____
_____

What do I want to get known for through my book?

_____

_____

_____

_____

_____

_____

_____

_____

What are my passions and talents?

_____

_____

_____

_____

_____

_____

_____

_____

_____

_____

_____

When you know and understand your ideal reader and client, it makes it easier to write to this one person in your book and tap into their wants, needs and desires.

My ideal client and reader is...

_____

_____

_____

_____

_____

_____

_____

_____

_____

_____

_____

_____

_____

_____

_____

_____

Consider aspects like their age, gender, personal situation.
Are they working, a stay-at-home mum/dad, retired, self-
employed, a leader or CEO? Where is your potential
reader in their life right now? Are they going through
change, such as empty nest syndrome, divorce, marriage,
retiring, college or university, starting or leaving a job,
redundancy, grief?

Their problem or objective is...

_____

_____

_____

_____

_____

_____

_____

_____

_____

_____

_____

_____

_____

_____

_____

_____

_____

_____

What problem do they need solving? What is their objective or what new information do they want from your book? What are they struggling with right now? What are they frustrated about? What are they moaning about with their colleagues or when out with their mates? What are they worrying about when they can't sleep? What are their biggest fears?

Through the book, I'll help them with this...

_____

_____

_____

_____

_____

_____

_____

_____

_____

_____

_____

_____

_____

_____

_____

_____

How are you going to help them? What stops them from making the change or difference that you can help them to make? What do they want instead? What will your book give them that they don't have already?

So that they achieve this result...

_____

_____

_____

_____

_____

_____

_____

_____

_____

_____

_____

_____

_____

_____

_____

_____

_____

_____

What is the solution or result that you'll help them to get once they've read your book? What is your big promise or outcome? How will your book help them to bridge this gap from where they are now to where they want to be?

Do I have a secondary or tertiary reader?

_____
_____
_____
_____
_____
_____
_____
_____
_____
_____
_____
_____
_____
_____
_____
_____
_____
_____

There may be other people who would benefit from reading your book who fall outside of your ideal client avatar. I call these people 'secondary' and 'tertiary' readers. These are people other than your 'ideal reader' who may find your book useful.

The next steps for my readers after reading my book

_____

_____

_____

_____

_____

_____

_____

_____

_____

_____

_____

_____

_____

_____

_____

_____

_____

Consider how you plan to leverage your book and what
you'd like your readers to do after they've read it. Does
it lead into a course, workshop, working with you one-to-
one? Do you want organisers to book you for speaking
engagements, your book to be recommended reading for
a course, or something else?

Space for additional notes

Space for additional notes

To-Do List

Date:

Done?	Item Name	Due Date

Principle 2
Choosing your
subject wisely

Choosing your subject wisely

When you decide what you're writing about *before* you put pen to paper, hands to keyboard, or voice to recording device, it will make it easier to write the right book for your business.

Over the years, I've seen many authors struggle in this area, because they try to shoehorn too many ideas into their book. Or they go to the other extreme of not having enough content to make it valuable. Or worse still, they pick the wrong subject for their audience.

In this section, the questions will drill down into your book's subject, enabling you to consider what you plan to share.

If you're like many business experts, you probably have lots of information that you could be talking about, so deciding how many books you're writing and what needs to go in *this* book is an important place to start.

Once you've explored your ideas, you will be prompted to identify what content your readers are most desperate to learn about and which of your ideas are going to benefit your business the most.

I also invite you to consider what market research you may undertake for your book. This may include carrying out a reader survey, interviews, social media posts, videos, blogs and having conversations with your ideal readers and clients.

All of these are great ways of building your profile, enabling you to self-fund it and self-validate your content as you write it.

If you've not yet watched the Masterclass where I explain these concepts in more detail, go and register to watch it here: www.librotas.com/smart-author.

How many books am I writing?

_____

What are these books about?

_____

_____

_____

_____

_____

_____

_____

_____

_____

_____

_____

_____

_____

_____

_____

_____

Which book do people want to hear about right now?

_____

_____

_____

_____

_____

_____

_____

_____

Which book do I want to write first?

_____

_____

_____

_____

_____

_____

_____

_____

_____

_____

_____

Which book will make the biggest impact right now?

Which book am I going to write first?

_____

_____

_____

_____

_____

_____

_____

_____

_____

_____

_____

_____

_____

_____

_____

_____

_____

_____

_____

_____

What market research do I need to do?

Doing market research is a great way to self-fund and self-validate your book as you write it, enabling you to find out what people want to hear from you and raise your profile at the same time. Use this opportunity to build a list of people who can't wait to buy it!

What are my next steps regarding market research?

Space for additional notes

Space for additional notes

To-Do List

Date:

Done?	Item Name	Due Date

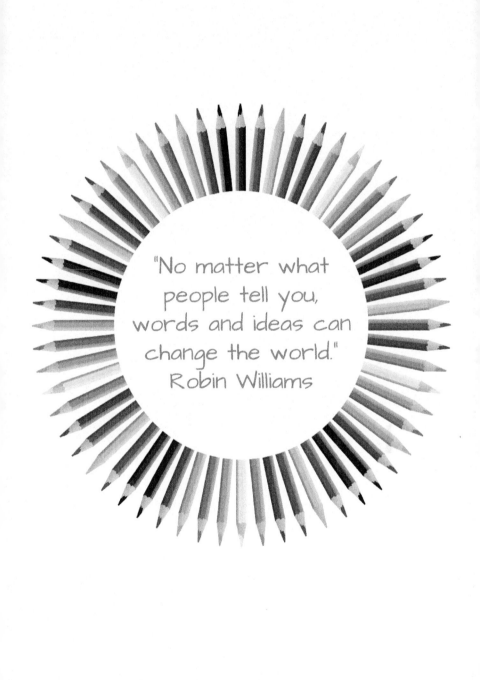

"No matter what people tell you, words and ideas can change the world."
Robin Williams

Principle 3
Finding your
secret sauce

Finding your secret sauce

The third principle is designed to help you find your magic. Your secret sauce.

This is the thing that makes you and your book unique, compared to every other book and author out there.

Many authors forget that they've got lots of competition, meaning that some end up churning out yet another book on a subject that's been done to death.

If your readers think they've read something similar before, and can't see why yours is different or is going to finally give them the answer they are looking for, they are unlikely to buy it.

In this section, I encourage you to start by considering your competitors' books. Pop into your local bookshop, online bookstore or check out 'Look Inside' on Amazon to get a feel for other books published and their content. You may already have some of these on your bookshelf.

Then once you know what you're competing against, you can start to tease out your hook, your angle and what you do that makes you unique.

This is time to dig deep and get clear on what makes you stand out from everyone else in your marketplace. If you're struggling in this area, take some time to review client testimonials or ask your colleagues what makes you different.

Please don't hold back here! This section will help you to become certain that your book will be seen as distinct, desirable and prove you are an authority in your area of expertise.

These are my competitors' books

These are my competitors' books (cont.)

What makes my book idea different?

What is my hook or unique angle?

What makes me different from my competitors?

_____

_____

_____

_____

_____

_____

_____

_____

_____

_____

_____

_____

_____

_____

_____

_____

_____

_____

_____

_____

This may include the number of years' experience you have in your industry, the clients/sectors you've worked with and the results they've achieved, your specialism and what you do well, awards and accolades, memberships of appropriate awarding bodies, and anything else that is relevant to your readers.

Why am I the best person to write this book?

_____

_____

_____

_____

_____

_____

_____

_____

_____

_____

_____

_____

_____

_____

_____

Consider here things like your life experiences or anything important about your journey or story, expertise, training, unique ideas, process or wisdom. It's time to brag!

Space for additional notes

Space for additional notes

To-Do List

Date:

Done?	Item Name	Due Date

Principle 4
Structuring
your book

Structuring your book

I love the fourth principle. This is where you will see your book rapidly forming right in front of your eyes!

But if you're wondering whether this section is worth your time, may I ask you a question... How many times have you given up on a book because the author jumps around from one idea to another? Books like this can be difficult to read and can feel disjointed or rambling.

This happens because most authors jump straight into writing the content before they've adequately planned out their ideas. If your book is not well structured, your reader is likely to end up confused and put your book down as not worth their time, which will do little to build your authority as an author, thought leader, or credible businessperson.

By contrast, one key benefit of a well-structured and planned book is that it's far easier and quicker to write. It will flow better and will be a nicer experience for your readers. This will increase the likelihood that they will leave you great reviews and want to work with you or recommend you in the future.

Firstly in this section, I suggest that you decide what type of book you are writing, as this will help you to structure your book.

Secondly, do you have a process, system or story that you share already that needs to form the outline of your book?

Then I recommend you use this space in your journal or on a big piece of paper, and map it out as a big colourful plan, either using Post-it notes or via a mind map.

Once you've explored your ideas, there is space to go deeper into the structure for each chapter, which will make it much easier when it gets to the next principle, when you start writing your book.

This is the book I am writing

_____

_____

_____

_____

_____

_____

_____

_____

_____

_____

_____

_____

_____

_____

_____

_____

Include on this page the type of book you are writing. Is your book a how-to guide or self-help book, an interview style book or a memoir? When you know this first, your book is more likely to flow and be easier to write!

This is the likely process, system or story I'll follow

Space for mapping out your book

Space for mapping out your book

Space for mapping out your book

Space for mapping out your book

Space for mapping out your book

Having a clear structure before you start to write your book will help you to make the most of your time.

Rather than staring at a blank page, wondering what to write, you will know exactly what's coming next and get on and write it!

My chapter outline and purpose of each chapter

CHAPTER NO.   CHAPTER OUTLINE AND PURPOSE

CHAPTER NO.   CHAPTER OUTLINE AND PURPOSE

My chapter outline and purpose of each chapter

CHAPTER NO.   CHAPTER OUTLINE AND PURPOSE

CHAPTER NO.   CHAPTER OUTLINE AND PURPOSE

My chapter outline and purpose of each chapter

CHAPTER NO.   CHAPTER OUTLINE AND PURPOSE

CHAPTER NO.   CHAPTER OUTLINE AND PURPOSE

My chapter outline and purpose of each chapter

CHAPTER NO.   CHAPTER OUTLINE AND PURPOSE

CHAPTER NO.   CHAPTER OUTLINE AND PURPOSE

My chapter outline and purpose of each chapter

CHAPTER NO.   CHAPTER OUTLINE AND PURPOSE

CHAPTER NO.   CHAPTER OUTLINE AND PURPOSE

Space for other notes, ideas or additional chapters

Space for other notes, ideas or additional chapters

Top writing tips

PREPARE IN ADVANCE

Plan non-negotiable writing time in your diary – treat your writing like a client.

SET A TIMER

Set a timer for 45 minutes to write. And set a timer for your rest period, so you don't get distracted!

SET UP YOUR WRITING ZONE

Set up a workspace where you are not going to be distracted or disturbed.

DECIDE YOUR FOCUS

Decide what you're going to focus on before you get started. A good plan will help.

SET BOUNDARIES

Set your boundaries with your loved ones and communicate the importance of your writing.

BE FLEXIBLE

Sometimes your writing won't go to plan and that's OK. Every baby step is a step towards your ultimate goal of writing your book.

To-Do List

Date:

Done?	Item Name	Due Date

Principle 5
Scheduling and
scribing

Scheduling and scribing

Now you've done the preparation, it's time to write your book!

It's easy to get stuck in the writing phase. But this is more likely to happen if you don't know who you are writing your book for, how it fits into your business, or you don't have a plan or structure to follow. However, this shouldn't be a problem for you if you've completed the previous sections.

Over the next few pages, you will explore how, when and where you can write at your best, because when you set yourself up for success, you're more likely to stick to your plan to achieve it.

And taking about your plan, I also include everything you need to think about when planning, writing, publishing and launching your book, so that you can work backwards from your proposed launch date and outline all the activities and the dates by which you wish to achieve these actions.

These include things like who you may ask to write the foreword for your book, how you plan to get published, and all the milestones on your book writing, publishing and marketing journey.

There's plenty of space for you to make notes, enabling you to use this journal as a resource to refer back to as you continue to get ready for your book launch and publication.

Please note that principles 6-8 will also help you to write your book and will feed into your plan, so be sure to complete these sections before you start to write the first chapter!

When do I write at my best?

_____
_____
_____
_____
_____
_____
_____
_____

Where do I write at my best?

_____
_____
_____
_____
_____
_____
_____
_____
_____
_____
_____
_____

Who can help me to write at my best?

_____

_____

_____

_____

_____

_____

_____

_____

How will I ensure my book is a priority?

_____

_____

_____

_____

_____

_____

_____

_____

_____

_____

_____

Book planning tool

Activity and actions	By when
Planning and development of ideas	
Research and interviews	

Book planning tool

Activity and actions	By when
Case studies and stories (principle 6)	
Expert tips and interviews (principle 6)	

Book planning tool

Activity and actions	By when
Book structure & synopsis (see final section for synopsis)	
Book marketing plan initiated	

Book planning tool

Activity and actions	By when
Completion of introduction	
First draft chapter 1 completed	

Book planning tool

Activity and actions	By when
First draft chapter 2 completed	
First draft chapter 3 completed	

Book planning tool

Activity and actions	By when
First draft chapter 4 completed	
First draft chapter 5 completed	

Book planning tool

Activity and actions	By when
First draft chapter 6 completed	
First draft chapter 7 completed	

Book planning tool

Activity and actions	By when
First draft chapter 8 completed	
First draft chapter 9 completed	

Book planning tool

Activity and actions	By when
First draft chapter 10 completed	
First draft of additional chapters completed	

Book planning tool

Activity and actions	By when
Self-edit of manuscript	
First review completed	

Book planning tool

Activity and actions	By when
Developmental edits completed (if required)	
Peer reviewers contacted (principle 8)	

Book planning tool

Activity and actions	By when
Draft ready for peer reviews (principle 8)	
Peer reviews started & completed (principle 8)	

Book planning tool

Activity and actions	By when
Title & subtitle finalised	
Foreword & reviews completed	

Book planning tool

Activity and actions	By when
Acknowledgements and/or dedication completed	
Copyright & references checked (principle 8)	

Book planning tool

Activity and actions	By when
Illustrations & graphics completed (if using)	
Back cover copy completed	

Book planning tool

Activity and actions	By when
Draft ready for editing & proofreading (principle 8)	
Editing & proofreading completed (principle 8)	

Book planning tool

Activity and actions	By when
Final draft ready for publication	
Revision of book marketing plan	

Book planning tool

Activity and actions	By when
Price decided for print & e-book (taking into account distribution & printing fees)	
Metadata completed (short/long description, categories & keywords)	

Book planning tool

Activity and actions	By when
Design agreed (internal typeset & cover design, principle 8)	
Publication of book – proposed date	

Book planning tool

Activity and actions	By when
Book launch date agreed & planned	
Post book launch marketing plan ready	

How will you make time to write your book?

Break down the activities into bite sized chunks, plan your completion date, schedule protected time in your diary, and get accountability to keep you on track.

Space for additional notes

Space for additional notes

Space for additional notes

To-Do List

Date:

Done?	Item Name	Due Date

Principle 6
Stories and
seeding

Stories and seeding

We have all got a story to tell that has led us to where we are today. And actually, most of us have multiple stories. But many people fail to share their story in their book, meaning that their readers don't realise how they can support them.

If you have been through devastating experiences and have learnt things the hard way, you will probably know that you have a story worth sharing. And even if you don't think your story is important, trust me, it is. So please be brave enough to tell it.

When you share your story, people get to know you as a person. If they have been through something similar, they will probably resonate with the highs and lows of your journey.

A good story, in my view, tugs on your heartstrings and taps into the emotions of what you've been through. So take some time to note these stories in this section.

The other thing you may wish to do is seed other people's stories and case studies in your book. People do love stories, especially when they are relevant and illustrate a particular point. But you will need to get permission before publishing.

Finally, you may also wish to have other experts contribute to your book or you may choose to interview people in specific areas.

There is space in this section to explore your ideas. You can add these to your plan when you're ready.

What is my story?

How am I going to include my story?

_____

_____

_____

_____

_____

_____

_____

_____

_____

_____

_____

_____

_____

_____

_____

_____

_____

In principle 4, I suggested that you decide what type of book you are writing, which will impact on how you share your story. If your book is memoir in style, it is likely to follow the 'hero's journey' approach and if your book is how-to in style, you may write a prologue or share parts of your story as and when it is relevant to the text.

Where am I an expert?

_____

_____

_____

_____

_____

_____

_____

_____

_____

_____

_____

_____

_____

_____

_____

_____

_____

_____

On the back cover of your book, you're likely to include your biography, which will summarise your experiences and expertise. Where are you an expert? What do your clients say that you're good at?

Case studies I wish to include in my book

Expert tips or interviews that I wish to include

Space for additional notes

Space for additional notes

To-Do List

Date:

Done?	Item Name	Due Date

"Either write something worth reading or do something worth writing."
Benjamin Franklin

Principle 7
Self-confidence

Self-confidence

When you write a blog or post on social media, it can be deleted. But the same can't be said about a book. Once it's in the public domain, there's no easy way of recalling the information, which can feel scary.

For many, when they write a book, they are putting their head above the parapet for the first time. Although this is a good thing business-wise, it can be daunting. Instead of impacting one person at a time, you're impacting multiple people at once.

When you put anything 'out there' for feedback, even at the research and writing stage, people will tell you what they think, and it's amazing what resistance we can come up against if we don't deal with it. You can be sure that staying stuck won't help you to get on and write it.

Self-confidence is something you can develop, and the more you get support and ask for feedback, the easier it will be to share what you know, and pick yourself up when the going gets tough.

So in this section, I advise you to consider how you can stay motivated, raise your confidence, and find your biggest cheerleaders.

And if you need help in this area, do get in touch. As with all of the areas covered in this planner, we do have team members who can help you to keep focused and stay on track.

In what areas might I struggle with self-confidence?

Where might I get stuck?

How can I get unstuck or increase my confidence?

How can I stay motivated?

_____

_____

_____

_____

_____

_____

_____

_____

_____

_____

_____

_____

_____

_____

_____

_____

_____

_____

_____

_____

Who will be my cheerleaders?

Space for additional notes

Space for additional notes

To-Do List

Date:

Done?	Item Name	Due Date

#SMARTAUTHORSYSTEM

Principle 8
Getting
support

Getting support

When you want your book to position you as an authority, don't do it alone. There are lots of moving parts to a book, so knowing what to do, when and how, will save you the stress of doing it all by yourself.

You may engage a book mentor, like me. I will help you with the strategy behind your book, its content and ensure it happens in a timely manner.

My role is to support you through the process of turning your ideas into a book that you are proud of, and give you feedback on your writing, so that you write a brilliant book. Plus I'll help with your marketing and launch.

The next step, when you get near the final draft, is to ask other people to give you feedback on your book – known as peer reviewers, which you will have seen earlier in the plan. Choose your reviewers wisely. Preferably they will be your ideal readers. They can help determine if you've pitched your book at the right level and whether there are any gaps or assumptions in your writing.

If you're publishing your book yourself, I advise you to engage a copy-editor and a proofreader who is CIEP (Chartered Institute of Editing and Proofreading) accredited. Apart from checking for errors at word and sentence level and ensuring your words flow as well as they can, they'll also be able to advise on where permission might be needed to use others' work and will be able to help you reference any material used in the right way.

You will also need a designer and publisher to help you to typeset the book, design the cover and ensure your book is published on all the e-book and print book platforms, ultimately enabling it to be easily distributed to your readers. Lastly, you need to market and sell your book – more on that in the final two principles.

We can help in all of these areas, so get in touch for support.

Who needs to be on my support team?

_____

_____

_____

_____

_____

_____

_____

_____

_____

_____

_____

_____

_____

_____

_____

_____

_____

_____

_____

_____

_____

Who will be my peer reviewers?

What is my publishing plan?

What references might I include in my book?

_____

_____

_____

_____

_____

_____

_____

_____

_____

_____

_____

_____

_____

_____

_____

_____

_____

You may reference books, articles, research, websites,
business models or other concepts in your book that
originate from other sources. Use this page to include
the details, so that you can refer back to it later.

What copyright permissions do I need to obtain?

If you are using other people's models and/or quotes in your book, you will need to seek permission to include them if this is beyond fair use, i.e. you are quoting a substantial chunk of someone else's work. You can note these down here to keep a record and make a note once permissions have been sought.

Who will write my foreword and review my book?

Space for additional notes

Space for additional notes

To-Do List

Date:

Done?	Item Name	Due Date

#SMARTAUTHORSYSTEM

Principle 9
Being savvy
about sales

Being savvy about sales

The worst thing you can do is spend your time and energy writing and publishing your book and then do nothing with it, or wait until the launch of your book to start talking about it.

It's important to stress here that however you decide to publish your book, most of the marketing – if not *all* of the marketing – will be down to you. Sure you might get some support or you might engage a team to help, but no one will be as committed to your book as you are!

That's why in the Smart Author System online programme and when people work with me one-to-one, I teach 7 ways you can self-fund your book as you write it, meaning that when you get to the publication stage, you will already have a hungry crowd of people who can't wait to get their hands on a copy.

It's also why I support people through the whole process, including the launch and making sure that they have a plan after they have published.

If you've not yet got my fifth book, *Book Marketing Made Simple*, then I suggest you get a copy. It's available at www.bookmarketingmadesimple.com and via all online bookstores.

This will help you to put together a plan to market your book at all stages of your book writing journey, from the day you start to write it, if not before, until way after you've launched your book.

In this section, I share some questions to get you started in thinking about how you can get savvy about sales!

What am I doing to promote my book as I write it?

_____

_____

_____

_____

_____

_____

_____

_____

_____

_____

_____

_____

_____

_____

_____

_____

_____

_____

_____

_____

What are my book launch plans?

What do I plan to do after my book is published?

_____

_____

_____

_____

_____

_____

_____

_____

_____

_____

_____

_____

_____

_____

_____

_____

_____

_____

_____

_____

_____

Use content from your book to create other content, such as podcasts, videos and blogs. This is an easy and effective way of sharing and repurposing your expertise and getting feedback on your ideas at the same time.

Space for additional notes

Space for additional notes

To-Do List

Date:

Done?	Item Name	Due Date

#SMARTAUTHORSYSTEM

Principle 10
Showing up in
a bigger way

Showing up in a bigger way

In my view, many authors face a big problem...

They will often choose to sit down and write their books because they are introverts.

They write their books because it's a safe space to show up. They can carefully take their time to craft their words and think about what they want to say before they say it.

But if you want to promote and sell your book, you have to tell people about it.

And even the most seasoned extroverts can struggle with this!

Although we are blessed with the advancement of technology, just sharing your book on social media isn't going to cut it.

Showing up is about telling people about your book in the right way. Like knowing where your ideal readers hang out so that you can reach them and getting help from other people in your sphere of influence to help you.

So with this final principle, I urge you to think about how you are going to show up, who can help you to get your book out to those who need to read it, and what's next on your book marketing plan.

How do I need to show up?

_____

_____

_____

_____

_____

_____

_____

_____

_____

_____

_____

_____

_____

_____

_____

_____

_____

_____

_____

_____

_____

Who could be my collaborators and connections?

How can they help me?

What podcasts, interviews, talks do I need to get on?

How will I step into my thought leadership?

_____

_____

_____

_____

_____

_____

_____

_____

_____

_____

_____

_____

_____

_____

_____

If you're using your book to establish you as a thought leader or expert, what else could you do to show up in a bigger way? This could include book awards, speaking, doing a TEDx talk or something else which raises your profile.

Space for additional notes

Space for additional notes

To-Do List

Date:

Done?	Item Name	Due Date

#SMARTAUTHORSYSTEM

"Ideas are like rabbits. You get a couple and learn how to handle them, and pretty soon you have a dozen."
John Steinbeck

Bringing it all
together

Bringing it all together

I hope you've found the *Business Book Planner* useful.

Over the coming few pages, I invite you to complete your synopsis, as this will help you to bring all of your thoughts together from some of the earlier work that you have done.

It will be great for you to see all of your hard work in one place!

Plus, this is perfect if you wish to pitch to a publisher or if someone asks you that all-important question: "Tell me more about your book…"

You'll also find a plan overview, which gives you an 'at a glance' overview of your entire plan, ready to write it.

If you haven't already got a copy of the accompanying journal – the *Book Writing Journal* – then you can get your copy from Amazon or via www.librotas.com today.

This is the perfect way to record all of your thoughts and ideas for your book as you write it, so that everything is all in one place. Or you may choose to sit down with the journal and write your book by hand.

Synopsis

Title, subtitle and short summary introduction

Synopsis

Chapter overview

Synopsis

Primary reader, secondary reader, tertiary reader

Synopsis

Competitor books

Synopsis

Biography/story

Synopsis

Marketing opportunities

Synopsis

Contact details and social media links

My book plan at a glance

Activity	Date
Initial plan complete	
Research and interviews completed	
Book structure and synopsis completed	
First draft of the book completed	
Self-edits completed	
Developmental edits completed	
Peer reviewers agreed	
Peer reviews completed	
Acknowledgements, reviews, foreword, back cover copy completed	
Draft ready for editing and proofreading	
Editing and proofreading completed	
Final draft ready for publication	
Internal design and cover agreed	
Other publication activities completed	
Book publication date	
Book launch date	
Marketing plan developed	

What's Next?

Thank you so much for working through this planner. I'd love to know how you got on. You can get hold of any of my books and the *Book Writing Journal* via Amazon or my website (www.librotas.com).

If you'd like additional support, here's how we can support you.

1. Book a Make It Happen day

Make It Happen days are designed to kick start your motivation. Whether you're getting started, or doing your planning, writing or editing, you'll join a small group of authors via Zoom for the day, and get advice, support and the chance to pick our brains to make your book happen. Dates and details can be found at www.librotas.com/make-it-happen.

2. Join the Smart Author System

The Smart Author System online training programme is where you can learn everything you need to write your book that enables you to self-validate and self-fund it as you write it. You can join the Self-study option or the Community version. The latter includes a Make It Happen day, Facebook community, expert interviews and additional support. Details can be found at www.librotas.com/smartauthor.

3. Apply for a one-to-one book mentoring programme

My one-to-one programmes are for leaders and experts who are passionate about making a difference through their book and are ready to step up and take massive action. Working with me personally, they get support every step of the way to write a book that raises their profile. Limited spaces available.

You can arrange a complimentary Book Focus call at www.librotas.com/contact.

About Karen Williams

Karen Williams is The Book Mentor at Librotas. She has worked with hundreds of business experts – coaches, therapists, leaders and consultants – who have a story to tell or a message to share.

She helps her clients to write, launch and market their best non-fiction book or memoir that increases their confidence, raises their credibility and attracts more clients, all of which enable them to stand out from the crowd and show up in a bigger way.

Her clients have achieved amazing successes, including becoming Amazon bestsellers and book award finalists, with high profile PR on *Woman's Hour* and in publications around the world, plus attracting new clients and launching successful courses off the back of their books.

After starting her business in 2006, Karen's own book writing journey began in 2009, and she is the bestselling author of *Becoming An Authority*, *Book Marketing Made Simple*, *The Mouse That Roars*, *Your Book is the Hook*, *How to Stand Out in Your Business,* and *The Secrets of Successful Coaches*.

She has contributed to numerous other books, is a TEDx speaker and regularly talks about business and book topics at networking groups, and features on podcasts and in the media. She works with a brilliant team who can support you through all stages of the book writing and publishing process.

Printed in Great Britain
by Amazon

61876244R00092